ALBERTO PINTO
WORLD INTERIORS

Julien Morel

Flammarion

Contents

The paradox of great interior design is that it is an art of the invisible, of choreographing the spaces between things to make them sing. Alberto is THE great master of this invisible art.

The moment we met we embraced each other's work and began a journey of discovery.

One of the great pleasures of being an artist is coming across your work unexpectedly, in a real-life interior. This is even more of a pleasure in one of Alberto's interiors.

The most important thing in life is the quality of our relationships with others. Internet, email, and mobile phones give us an almost continuous means of communication.

Because of that we can lose sight of the fact that the really profound connections between people happen when we occupy the same space.

A consequence of our virtual downloadable world is that the undownloadable unique experiences like art and interiors get rarer and rarer.

This is why Alberto's work is so important—simply put, he creates the spaces where real life happens.

Alberto is always in the moment, reflecting and refracting; he is like the most beautiful prism, turning the white light of the everyday into the beautiful colors of the worlds he designs.

We only live once: best to live that life in Pintoworld!

Walking into an interior created by Alberto Pinto is a rare privilege, one that belongs to a cosmopolitan circle of wealthy individuals who ask him to decorate their environment without betraying their personality, nor letting him impose his. A keen observer of mankind and of objects, the French decorator is skilled in understanding the singularity of each person, and draws instinctively on the threads of original decorative scenes from those commissioning his work.

From his role as an outside observer is born the distinctiveness of his designs, producing a change of scene for each interior that is at once surprising and natural. Disregarding fashions or styles, the only thing that counts is the lasting pleasure that will be felt by the person who inhabits the place once the work is finished. They should find the idealized vision of an island, an incomparable image of a distant paradise of lands ruled in perfect harmony. An ecosystem that juxtaposes a society of useful forms in the service of comfort, a bestiary of animated objects imbued with the spirit of diverse cultures, and collects works gleaned from a vast imaginary garden to form a made-to-measure Eden for its inhabitants. This dream is like his creations, flourishing as rare orchids whose simplicity is never neutral and whose sophistication is innate.

The pages of this eighth book on the work of Alberto Pinto set out to discover some of these places in a well mapped-out itinerary defined by the mark of excellence. The work takes us to destinations in Mexico, the Caribbean, Monaco, to exceptional houses in New York and Kuwait, and into the corridors of important businesses. Transformations are to be seen on board super-yachts and private jets. Along each step of the journey described in this book, a unique creative horizon opens up.

In a newly created palace one finds the quintessence of orientalism. In a nineteenth-century town house one finds classical codes mixed with modernity. A beach house becomes a setting for a collection of eclectic art. All the projects provide examples of a research into originality that knows no bounds. The presentation of three different possibilities for the arrangement of an airplane is significant. In this area, governed by the constraints of space and by draconian airline standards, Alberto Pinto succeeds in finding original methods that reveal in turn the expression of a dynamic design, the comfort of an English club, or even a delicate feminine refinement.

The wide scope of these projects reveals an astonishing capacity for renewal, its underlying layer being an inexhaustible culture. Alberto Pinto eschews the rigidity of textbooks to find his sources in the rich life experiences of a "grand tour" begun in his childhood, growing up on both sides of the Mediterranean. The sun of Casablanca and the rigor of Paris form a founding contrast to his aesthetic experience, cultivated afterwards in his studies at the École du Louvre and through his first professional experience as publishing director for the Condé Nast group. Enthusiast before becoming trendsetter, early on Alberto Pinto acquired, almost compulsively, objects that seduced him. Beautiful things look beautiful together and the eyes of Alberto Pinto unfailingly distinguish the superior characteristic of a piece. He assesses it by the quality of its material, the subtlety of a line, the originality of its subject, the skill and expertise involved, or simply the curiosity that it incites. The inventory of mysteriousness which underpins the sense of beauty, and whose criteria evade the classification of styles, is inexhaustible. As an expert, discovering as much in the contemporary world as in that of the ancient, Alberto Pinto declares the eclecticism of his choices as an intellectual liberty, a deep defiance with regard to boredom, or in terms of a "total look." This last detail explains his refusal to repeat the same schemes. Even to speak about it would be an absurdity. There are no two spheres that he views in the same manner, nor are there the same demands twice: he sets himself the challenge of seeking out the differences. As an interior architect for his own projects before working for others, Alberto Pinto is a self-taught individual guided by a passion, one who conceives his decors as a designer would his or her collections. A guiding principle gives them coherence; like a spool that unravels its last thread, prompting him to start a new one. Impelled forward from the moment of his first projects, Alberto Pinto knew that he had to return to Paris in order to satisfy his high standards. The French capital, in fact, brings together master craftsmen and -women capable of carrying out the completion of the interiors that he imagines. There are sculptors, painters, cabinetmakers, metal-smiths, plasterers, carpenters, saddlers, embroiderers, and soft-furnishing manufacturers, all indispensable accessories to his desire to merge perfection with reality.

The Hôtel de la Victoire, headquarters of Alberto Pinto's studio, is today at the epicenter of this school of excellence. A tour of this place, source of some forty projects being worked on simultaneously throughout the world, reveals certain principles dear to Alberto Pinto: the transparency of the spaces; their precise characterization; the emergence of art and of the living. It is a luminous workspace, comfortable and elegant, but also a place where Albert Pinto's art of living and art of creation can be expressed. Its entrance sets the tone: simple and majestic, it makes use of the perspective that opens up under the main

Facing page: One of the most celebrated French decorators, Alberto Pinto heads an agency in the heart of Paris that brings together eighty collaborators. The team has been assembled to accomplish a singular mission in terms of decoration; their goal is to propose totally individual environments. Around the world, he creates exceptional designs for grand homes, for contemporary lofts, for office buildings, for super-yachts, or for private airplanes.

Above and facing page: The Hôtel des Victoires was renovated by Alberto Pinto as a place of constant creation; the interior is marked by the taste of the decorator for the eclecticism of objects and the linking of epochs. A veritable hothouse of decorative solutions, his agency brings together samples from a multitude of suppliers: experts in fabrics, in cabinetry, and in the weaving of wood, as well as materials with innovative finishes. Meticulously inventoried in baskets or on panels, they are juxtaposed on style boards that are composed for projects under development. Enlarged in 2011, Alberto Pinto's studio and agency began a new department devoted to luxury hotels, an area which has seen constant expansion, allowing Alberto Pinto to extend his research into exclusivity and excellence, driven by forty years of experience, even further.

gateway to support the presence of a large bronze, flanked by two magnolias that take root in the high gardens. The architectural nobility of the building, dating from the seventeenth century, is itself soberly shown off by the Renaissance-inspired frescos that grace the porch.

On the floor, the checkerboard of white and black stone immediately reveals the prestigious footprints of a great house. It is only the presence of a piece of furniture carefully wrapped up, awaiting shipment, that betrays the activity of a hive where works are permanently waiting to be transported. An African throne covered in pearls sleeps under the eye of a Victory in bronze that watches over the foot of a grand staircase, the backbone of the building leading to the various levels. The epicenter is on the second floor, and it is on this level that one finds the office of Alberto Pinto and the grand showroom that he often uses as a workspace. At once *salon* to welcome clients and partners and a room for meetings with his close collaborators, it is also a library and an archive, with dozens of baskets filled with swatches and samples of cloth. It is a vast space allowing collaborators to come together for a final approval of the proposed elements of an interior.

The pulse of the agency beats between this room and the office on the other side of the courtyard. This initiates a very fertile dialogue between interior development and constructive exchange, while the beating heart pumps out directorial lines and instructions to the upper floors. Prescient interpretations of the desires outlined by clients, ideas are drawn in watercolor or in "travelings," modeled in 3D; these make up a succession of original views whose smallest detail, the embroidery of a door pull, for example, will be specifically conceived for the project for which it is destined. From initial drawings to the final product, a team of seventy collaborators works in an organized fashion in order to achieve in an efficient manner the intentions set out by Alberto Pinto. Aviation, corporate, residences, yachts: these four specialist departments of the studio witnessed the addition in

2011 of a fifth, concentrating on hotels, created after enlarging the office space. These various fields of competence are supported by a documentation center in which the details of over five thousand different suppliers are kept. In addition, an enormous archive housed in the attic, a real memorial treasure trove, bears witness to forty years of solutions, tried and tested on building sites. The breadth of skills and of resources converges to create, on the basis of an internationally acclaimed expertise, the world of dreams shown in this book.

Since 2010, part of this know-how has been more widely distributed by the "Pinto Paris" brand, which has produced a small series of collections of furniture, objects, accessories, and tableware created by Alberto Pinto for his projects. Presented behind showroom windows, open by appointment on the Rue de Mail and the Rue d'Aboukir in Paris, these collections allow people to get close to the art de vivre in whose service Alberto Pinto showcases all of his decors. An art de vivre that is obviously not absent from the Hôtel de la Victoire, where Alberto Pinto has renovated a dining room looking out onto a courtyard. Surrounded by contemporary artworks, the table is laid with a service from Limoges, painted by hand with graceful motifs or striking subjects designed for his collections. Around them, the silverware is different every day, as are the crystal ware and the bouquets of flowers, chosen to accompany the menu concocted by the head chef. The place mats are made of straw, and in this contrast one finds the essence of Alberto Pinto's style: a virtuoso who knows when to elicit a daring encounter with different kinds of materials. In this ephemeral environment, built around a meal, even more so than in his structural designs, the escape offered by the colors, the forms, the objects, and their uses, is rendered palpable. Alberto Pinto has been seeking out the ingredients all his life in the most faraway countries, as in literature or cinema, for this voyage of the spirit. There are fragments of a well-traveled humanity that he reunites in the Hôtel de la Victoire, as in his designs, like the many horizons that are revealed in the pages of this book.

Above and facing page: Built in the seventeenth century and a short walk from the garden of the Palais Royal, the Hôtel de la Victoire is the headquarters for Alberto Pinto's studio and agency and yet it retains the cachet of a grand city mansion. The decorator succeeds in preserving its authenticity, effortlessly creating a balance between functionality and prestige. The grand staircase, the backbone of the building, leads to the various floors of the offices. It illustrates the magnitude of the dimensions of the space, where modernity is sublimated by the eclecticism of the furniture and the works of art as this painting by Pierre Dmitrienko (above left).
Pages 12–13: The office of Alberto Pinto

Mexico: A Beach Apartment

With views extending to the horizon, this apartment, conceived as a summer holiday home for a contemporary art lover, boasts direct access to the beach. This proximity realizes the dream of a refuge at water's edge, shared by all those who have a taste for the infinite.

Facing the sea, the architecture reveals a fabulous panorama over the bay, toward which Alberto Pinto naturally chooses to set his decorative scene. He achieves this by emptying out a maximum of space, selecting simple decorative materials, and reducing the border between the interior and the exterior to its essential expression.

To ensure the full clarity of space, his first intervention consisted of pushing out the walls. The original structure was far from his own vision of a decent space: he succeeded in enlarging a suffocating terrace and expanded the living room to his desired size. The walls are covered with bands of textured white stucco, amplifying this effect, and allowing the zones of comfort to reach Hollywood proportions, all on a parquet flooring of Ipê wood with straw rugs.

The clearness of style marries with the blinding light of the summer, but is calmed by the unveiling of pure colors. He has created a sober palette that engages in the construction of a continuous dialogue between the sophisticated and the natural, allowing clever connections to emerge. An ivory tortoise at the bottom of a staircase, a silver frog by Luis Ferreira ready to jump up on a table, the sinuous dance of screeching monkeys, frozen in the bronze of a pedestal table by Claude Lalanne, or the double coconuts turned into sculptures—all combine to inhabit the space with surprising vitality.

A burst of bright colors plays a role as well. They spatter from the palette of an exuberant bouquet painted by Marc Quinn, in the abstraction of a sculpture by Jean-Claude Farhi, or in the ceremonious and colorful columns of Guy de Rougemont, set against the somber and tortured remains of a tree ripped up by its limbs, created by the Brazilian artist Frans Krajcberg.

In this land of fantasy, Asian antiques—which could have been brought by a Manila galleon, making its fortune in the New World of the seventeenth century, trading its treasures from the Far East—make an appearance. An element of mystery goes hand in hand with the most contemporary creations, suggesting a fertile circulation of goods over the ages, animated by vivid and ephemeral outbursts, in the same vein as the thousands of butterfly wings that enshroud the dining room in the evening.

That feeling of lightness, which reigns during vacation periods and in the summer, transforms into a feeling of escape in an interior decor that eludes the confines of space and invites reverie.

Page 14

The inspiration of nature is the central theme of the decor in this collector's apartment. In a corner of the living room, a pedestal table by Claude Lalanne rests on a stand of light bronze depicting several monkeys frozen in dance. It supports a sculpture of double coconuts, from which emerge an African fetish and a shaft of golden wheat.

Lef and facing page

A large bay window and glass railings allow a panoramic view of the ocean in this big living room divided into two spaces, the larger of which takes on a Hollywood-style grandeur. A painting by Marc Quinn and a sculpture in Plexiglas by Farhi display resplendent colors, livening up the natural neutrality of the setting.

Pages 18–19
An ivory tortoise watches over
the comings and goings of guests
between two salons, two spaces
defined by large coir rugs set off from
the parquet of light Ipê. Between a pair
of fake antique Thai pots raised on high
stands, a large abstract work by Nancy
Grave dominates a sofa, in front of
which stand a small lacquered table and
a banquette in the form of a black bean.

Facing page and right
Hieratic totems by Guy de Rougemont
under the stainless-steel meander
of the staircase; a large sculpture
in burnt wood by the Brazilian artist
Frans Krajcberg (behind the bar counter);
bronze busts by Darbaud on an Italian
console table: works of art are
omnipresent, set off from the simply
decorated walls by alternating strips
of white stucco.

Above and facing page
The remarkable burst of color of thousands of butterfly wings enshroud this dining room. The walls are completely covered by panels made from this fragile and precious material, based on designs by Alberto Pinto. The light given off from the alabaster lamp accentuates the charm and adds to the magic of the dinners for six gathered at a round table with chairs by Robsjohn-Gibbins.

Pages 24–25
In a corridor, a Burmese buddha in wood seems to be levitating against a opal glass wall that captures the light of the inner courtyard. On each side of a door, placed on art deco console tables, a pair of Thai deer in bronze are set back from a wall covered in cerused wood.

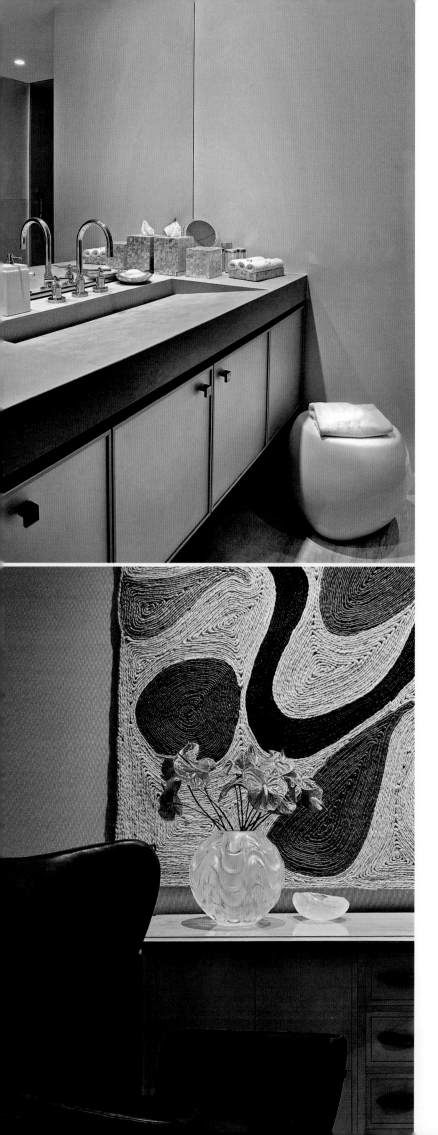

Left and facing page
A large tapestry by Calder hangs
over a dresser from the 1940s lined
in parchment in this room highlighted
in red. The color is picked up again in
the leather of the wing chairs and in the
parallel strips at the head of the bed.
Red is also found in the white chiné
on the coir rug and it lacquers the doors
of the cabinet and of the small chest
of drawers from the 1950s. On either
side of the bed, pedestal tables in gilded
bronze are topped by mirrored bases on
which are placed Murano glass lamps.
Above the dressing table by Porteneuve,
the drawing is by Francesco Clemente,
while four sketches by Yves Saint
Laurent hang at the end of the corridor.

Left

Above a lacquered and parchment desk from the 1940s, a mirror by Jean Royère, hung horizontally, reflects the twin beds in a small bedroom. The sky-blue cotton of the headboards and the chair cover lend freshness to the room. They blend with the green leather of the French bedside lamps, as well as the Murano glass bowl on the desk.

Above

In interiors by Alberto Pinto, bathrooms always have a special dimension. Here, the space is doubled by a very large mirror that reaches the ceiling. The sink is formed by a simple slope carved out of a long slab of reconstituted stone laid on top of a suspended black lacquered unit. A sculpture in bronze, evoking the work of Lucio Fontana, is placed in counterpoint to the empty space.

Left and facing page

On the large terrace that gives access directly to the beach, the heat of the sun is tempered by the luxury of a wall of orchids and by the comfort of a countercurrent swimming pool, allowing guests to refresh themselves without having to reach the shore. All of the furniture is in teak chosen at Sutherland's. It is perfectly adapted to the constraints of the interior, as in the cushions by Pierre Frey after an original design by Alberto Pinto. In echoes of maritime legends, two marble busts of mermaids serve to hold up lamps that illuminate nighttime conversations.

Left
On the first floor, the terrace has been enlarged by means of a mirror in front of which is laid a large ammonite fossil. Four simple cubes in teak are aligned in the axis of its spiral, like a minimalist installation, allowing them to be used as stools or as occasional tables. The two armchairs in teak, matched with large cushions, are by Sutherland; the fabric was designed by Alberto Pinto for Pierre Frey.

Above
Purchased from young artists on a neighboring beach, several square paintings inspired by the world of comic strips are hung along the staircase, while on the landing chirp the vivid colors of a fragile tree of birds in Murano glass.

Facing page and above
On the painted wall, the elegant *Dame en Noir* by Alexander Roubtzoff assures the master of the house a good night's rest. She seems to be supported by the Bull-Bench by the Parisian Jean-Marie Fiori, which sits at her feet on a coir rug. The furniture is rare and precious, as in the mirrored art deco writing desk or the alabaster standing lamp, topped by a lampshade in raw silk. On the headboard of the bed covered in toile de Tours, small trinkets are pinned, serving a protective as well as a decorative purpose.

Pages 36–37
Above the large desk sheathed in leather, the scene of the painting reminds us that we are in a bathroom. This reconciliation of uses—which breaks with conventions in order to marry a style of living with the obligations of the business world—is like the call of inspiration: it never ceases.

Left and facing page
The entrance to an enormous shower whose water falls like rain separates the exterior of the terrace from the very comfortable bathroom with dressing area. It encapsulates perfectly the demands of seaside living and trips from the beach. Under a drawing of a mermaid by Marc Quinn, a large chaise longue invites the owner to rest or to read while drying off. Enveloped by the calming softness of a thick rug and by walls covered in cerused wood, one can reflect on the right choice of wardrobe for the day. The laundry is methodically stored behind the serene, muted tones of panels of wood, or in the baskets of straw and leather lined with white cotton. A Dagobert chair covered in crocodile by Claude Lalanne takes its place—like an elegant night valet—in front of a stone vanity unit, topped by a mirror up to the ceiling and framed by two wall lights by Hervé van der Straeten.

Facing page and right

A television room takes its place
behind large screens in the living room.
The screens form an alcove where
a deep and comfortable banquette
nestles; on this are placed various
cushions covered in Punjabi silk.
The few pieces of furniture are
sculptures, as in a mirror by Hubert
Le Gall that reflects in its circles the
contemporary painting by Nicholas
Krushnick, which is itself crisscrossed
by orange diagonal lines that diffuse
the color of the cushions in the space.
A small guest room is treated with
great sobriety. The walls are painted
in a very soft, washed-out blue, set
off by the yellow fabric that covers
the headboard. The two gilded bedside
tables are the creations of Oppenheim
for Simon International. They are
topped by black ceramic lamps.
In front of the lacquered secretary,
the only important piece in the room,
a painting by Fassianos evokes the
theme of love. At the foot of the bed,
a Suzani throw brings the sun of the
Orient closer to the sun of Central
America. The adjacent bathroom is,
as always with Alberto Pinto's designs,
a spacious extension to the decorative
scheme of the room.

Pages 42–43

In this professional laboratory kitchen,
and around its central island made
from Corian®, the space and the
appliances in stainless steel and black
lacquer facilitate the organization of
receptions for numerous guests.

Manhattan:
A Large Family Apartment

A return to its roots for this prestigious three-story apartment in a nineteenth-century town house overlooking Central Park. Divided over the years into several apartments, the building today, according to the wishes of one of Alberto Pinto's most faithful clients, is gradually being restored to its original splendor under his care.

In a striking coincidence, revealing the historical magnetism of the high-end of the French decoration tradition, this project found Alberto Pinto following in the footsteps of the Frenchman Allard, a designer who first decorated this building in 1885. His legacy was an upper-level floor containing a number of ornamental elements, such as plaster moldings and wood paneling. Saved from reckless restorations, Alberto Pinto reinterprets the space with a real freshness in order to delimit elegant reception areas.

The antique furniture and the paintings by masters on the walls were patiently collected over time by the owners, often under the watchful eye of Alberto Pinto, integrating naturally into the majestic surroundings. They are joined by new elements giving an effect of grace and wonderment. Among these are an impressive collection of blue-and-white Chinese porcelain which adorns the high walls of the entry gallery. This forms a prelude; from here the large living room and the old library, now transformed into dining room, radiate.

From floor to floor, the choice of lightness takes one toward paths of modern refinement. On the upper floors, given over to the family bedrooms, a feeling of intimacy replaces that of grandeur. The parents' bedroom and that of the twin daughters evoke the serene atmosphere of a summer sky, impregnated by a feminine softness, to which is added the contrast of a concern for restraint. This moderation can be found in the modern layout of the top floor, which is divided between guest rooms and a cozy family room; a space given over to a playroom, favoring privacy and comfort. Under the watchful eyes of a series of Warhol Marilyns, the family meets here informally, while the codes of luxury are retained in the choice of beautiful materials and in the immaculate details: bookcases in braided wood, light fabrics used on the cushions, with the meander of an embroidery duplicated in the blinds, a sculpted carpet specially made. The deep sofas invite one to plunge into a film or a book, while a small dining area hosts snack times and serves as a place for homework.

In the heart of the bustling city, a nest is made to suit every mood, every need; from one in the formal language of representation to one, intimate and familiar, of the everyday.

Page 44
The entryway is on a monumental scale. The nobility of its dimensions is magnified by the carpet of marble on the floor, the pilasters, and the cornices in plaster mesh. But its theatricality comes from the rich display of blue-and-white Chinese porcelain found in the wreck of the *Ca Mau*, a ship from the East India company that sank in the eighteenth century.

Pages 46–47
The grand living room underwent a major, restoration that has softened the space, thanks to a subtle contrast of white and Wedgwood blue.

Left and facing page
Highlighted by satins from the house of Prelle, rewoven using instructions from original documents, the family collection is displayed in graceful tranquility: a large painting by Jacques-Émile Blanche; a fantasy armchair in gilt wood whose armrests are sculpted seahorses; a large chandelier with tassels; a herringbone cabinet; a low table in the style of Madeleine Castaing.

Facing page and right
The antechamber of the dining room takes the form of a rotunda with four corners. Illusory of bookcases hide the china cabinet designed to hold dinnerware. An English nineteenth-century pedestal table finds its place at the center of the rosette of the parquet floor; above it hangs a large Russian chandelier.

Pages 52–53
The formal dining room is surrounded by the restored wood paneling that is subtly set off by gold threads in echoes of the old library. The light is particularly beautiful here at the end of the day. It reflects the pearly sheen of the ivory silk damask of the curtains, shimmers in the old mirrors, carves out the outlines of the two marble busts from the eighteenth century, and shows off the brilliance of the night-blue enamel plaques of the two Russian chandeliers.

Facing page
The parents' bedroom unites the feminine softness found in the lace shades, the wall coverings, and the curtains—in blue cotton fabric re-embroidered with tiny ivory leaves—with the masculinity of the Biedermeier furniture. The elegance is as precious as it is austere in the large architectural wardrobe and in the finesse of the pedestal table with legs in the shape of swans, which come across even more vividly in this simple yet exquisite setting, as do the finesse of the embroideries and the stripes on the back of the chaise longue.

Above
A unity of style is respected in terms of the furniture in the bedroom: many pieces have been restored, allowing them to regain their original brilliance.

Left

Bathrooms occupy a special place
in the work of Alberto Pinto. This one
brilliantly illustrates the importance
that he gives to this space. Around
the large bathtub, the sinks are tucked
into identical niches decorated
in a modern Biedermeier style.
The adjoining dressing room continues
this theme in a very restrained way,
with the aim of maximizing comfort.

Facing page

The perspective of the bathroom is
interrupted by a comfortable armchair.
Natural light streams onto the light
sycamore wood, which is framed
by a more somber stained sycamore.
This contrast is repeated in the light
marble flooring with black cabochons.

Facing page
A long corridor separates the parents'
bedroom from that of the twin
daughters. Medallions in Sèvres biscuit
porcelain punctuate the walls, which
are covered with a blue cotton fabric
re-embroidered with white flowers,
identical to those used in the bedroom.
In the bedroom, small Princess
canopies are arranged on either side
of a mahogany bookcase, topped
by a gilded, wood-framed mirror.

Right
In the bathroom, the pink Norwegian
marble complements the seedbed
of the roses on the large English rug
of the bedroom. The bedroom is
discreetly appointed in order to give
maximum freedom for play. A simple
sofa and a small chest of drawers
adorn a room that is primarily given
over to the colors of the sky.

Left
On the level of the living room, where a table by Robert Kuo is used for dining, there is a also guest bedroom decorated in various shades of beige, based on inspirations of the 1950s and 1960s. These are recognizable in the design of the armchairs, the bedside tables in lacquer and parchment, but also in the drawing embroidered on the wool satin of the bed throw, specially created by Alberto Pinto.

Facing page
The low parchment and ebony table in the family room is a creation by Alberto Pinto, on which are placed a collection of Japanese objects mixed with pieces from the 1930s: on the two beige tweed sofas on either side of it are throw cushions embroidered by Holland and Sherry, whose motifs are also found on the blinds.

Pages 62–63
A silkscreen of Marilyn Monroe by Andy Warhol brings a pop touch to the ivory atmosphere of this comfortable living space.

Facing page
The second suite is a guest room and
keeps to the same principle: a sober
and contemporary design. Grays and
whites dominate, repeated in stripes,
in solid or in geometric patterns, on
flannel fabrics underlined by a red strip.
This touch of primary color prevents
the decor being seen as neutral.
Red punctuates the headboard, which
is sewn with square buttons, and
the bedside tables, and determines
the choice of lithographs by Aki Kuroda
from the Galerie Maeght.

Above
The adjoining bathroom is decorated
in a pronounced New York style.
It is entirely covered in slabs of white
marble veined in gray, with the exception
of the sink unit, which combines chrome
metal with frosted glass.

BBJ Private Jet: Design Takes Flight

The vigor of a clear line finds itself—on board this Boeing—reducing the distances between elegant design and superlative comfort. Ordered by a self-made man from Australia, it boasts a sober appearance and a masculinity true to its owner's desires.

To transform a 737, which in its commercial version can welcome 120 persons on board, into a plane for only twelve passengers, allows certain liberties to be taken. Alberto Pinto, who has over the last ten years become an expert in the refitting of private airplanes, shows us just that: this jet has been designed down to the smallest of details; nothing here comes from the pages of a catalog. Like many other projects led by his agency, it is through an attentive understanding of the needs of his client that Alberto Pinto imagines the lines, the materials, and the colors that bring together this remarkable plane.

For the owner, whose business doesn't wait and who carries out deals in the four corners of the world, the plane is as much a place of work as it is a necessary haven for rest. The decorator knows, nevertheless, that when refurbishing of an airplane, style and comfort are but one part of the group of parameters that must be taken into consideration. Functionality, acoustics, lighting, home automation—all these are also studied with care and attention, even if their high level of completion will disappear under the care of an individual and supreme aesthetic. This is made possible by the use of quality materials like leather and wood, which are omnipresent, but also by the detailing in metal chrome that adds to the general appearance, supported by the graphic design of the decoration.

The tour begins in the kitchen set aside for the crew, the galley, which sets the tone of rigor and of refined luxury, with elements in brushed metal and a Corian countertop.

The passengers are welcomed into a series of rooms that stand out in the perspective of space. Two large sofas face each other in the main cabin, providing a calming atmosphere. The solid-color carpet matches not only the beige chenille fabric that covers the seats, but also the squares of leather covering the partitions. Piping, headrests, blinds, and cornices in black leather stretch out the perspective toward an adjustable table for four where meals are served. There follows a second room, furnished with a large daybed and a desk, before reaching the more private part of the plane. A large bedroom boasts a double bed. The adjoining bathroom removes any feeling of confinement that a plane might create. In this setting of black marble, a large rectangular shower with ceiling "rain" showerhead washes away the tensions and allows one to forget that one is 12,000 feet up in the air.

The art of creation and of design is also to bring to the interior of a place the possibility of escape.

Page 66
The placement of seats and of sofas
structures the space of the main cabin.
It leaves space for a corner office and
for various rooms whose arrangement
breaks the linearity of the space with
a graphic effect supported by the contrast
of beige, black, and bright nickel.

Left and facing page
The quality of the material and the finishes
captures the eye. The seats, finished off
with leather piping, are upholstered in
saddle-stitched leather or in dyed black
cream velour. The carpet is silk. The lolo
wood is used in three different finishes,
enhanced by bright nickel inserts.

Pages 70–71
The cabin opens on to a perspective
of comfort, supported by vanishing lines
traced by the cornice and the decorative
blinds in saddle-stitched black leather.

Left and facing page
Fine china, silverware, crystal glasses; the table is set with tableware and household linens created by Alberto Pinto, who oversees every accessory in his conversions. Dinner for four people can be served here around a table that is fully adjustable. It can turn into a low table once cleared. The configuration also transforms the space into a comfortable corner in which to watch television, thanks to a television that is set into the beige suede-covered partition. The cupboards and the storage compartments in the corridor are in lolo veneer stained with gray or black lacquer. They serve as a cloakroom and stowage. The most fragile pieces of tableware are put away in the padded compartments.

Facing page

The office area, with its incorporated display, is attached to the back of a large day bed. The foam of the black leather desk chair, enhanced with beige piping, is adapted to the shape of the owner. This ergonomic engineering is linked to a search for optimal comfort, as much physical as visual, as in the choice of a precious lamp/sculpture or of the throw cushions. This constant ability to please the eye comes from the coherence of a project that is designed down to the finest details in Alberto Pinto's studio: he is as concerned with the global qualification of space as with the creation of magazine racks.

Right

The criteria of comfort and luxury are applied to the whole of the airplane: shown here is a seat for one of the crew members.

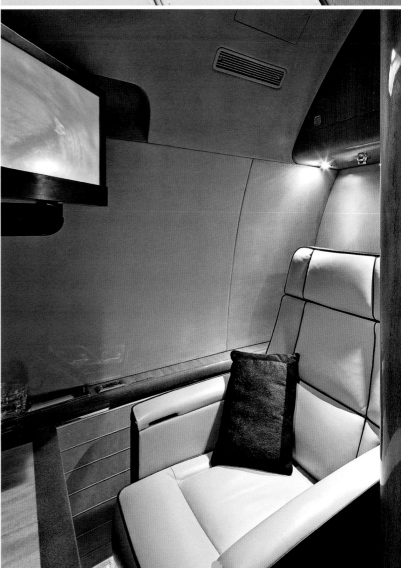

Left
All the elements of a professional kitchen are integrated in this ultra-compact galley where the use of Corian and of brushed metal gives a marked clarity of line and of surface.

Above
The quality and the placement of various lighting perspectives are evident in this photograph taken between the front lounge and the back lounge of the cabin, where magazine racks were designed to hide the doors of the supplementary storage spaces.

Facing page

The back of the plane is given over
to a spacious bedroom equipped with
a king-size bed whose base is covered
in topstitched black leather. It seems
to float on large drawers where the chrome
reflections resonate with the border
that encloses the design of the door
in varnished lolo. The walls are in beige
topstitched suede with horizontal lines
that reinforce the effect of perspective,
doubly underlined by the cornices and
the decorative blinds. In the adjoining
bathroom is a large, rectangular shower
with rain-type ceiling showerhead and
teak flooring.

Right

The sink recessed into the slab of black
marble is of chromed stainless steel.
Set within the bedside table are the
remote controls.

Caribbean Sea: The *Ocean Victory* Yacht

Only a handful of super-yachts, nautical titans of over 164 feet (50 m.), see the light of day every year. Exceptional in so many ways, they are particularly so in their conversion and decoration; here, pure creation and exclusivity are kings. Balancing a free rein in terms of inventiveness and the constraints of made-to-measure are familiar issues for Alberto Pinto. He is therefore particularly at ease in appropriating—according to the taste of his clients—bridges and passageways, rooms and cabins, spaces where he applies particular codes, not wanting to replicate at sea what one finds on land.

The temptation to transpose them in the renovation of a 246-foot (75-m.) yacht like the *Ocean Victory* is great; here is an exceptional ship, conceived by Feadship, whose spaces would satisfy the needs of those seeking a very large apartment. A number of decorators have crashed up against the reef of imitation. Alberto Pinto sidesteps this by inventing specific formulas for these exceptional vessels, taken from the unfathomable richness of his nautical imagination.

It is certainly for this reason that the shipowner, as passionate as he is demanding, called on Alberto Pinto. Very much involved in the project, he has found in Alberto Pinto an able man who was capable not only of interpreting his desires but also of seeing them through. His taste was closer to an expression of a non-ostentatious luxury, with an atmosphere that reflected family life. Thus, the ship, largely open to the outside, nonetheless has a protective ambience which allows its passengers to face the inevitable harsh elements.

By maintaining an overall stylistic unity, Alberto Pinto unveils a program of subtle modulations that play on a very large palette of quality materials, of warm colors, and of sophisticated finishings. Audaciously refusing not to replicate the worn classics of pairing wood with fabric, the decorator employs different essences and frameworks for each space on this vast vessel.

In memory of the cruise ships of the grand epoch—*"maisons superlatives"* (superlative houses), as Roland Barthes described them in his *Mythologies*, the *Ocean Victory* rivals the spaciousness of the villas on the coast. It can comfortably welcome fourteen passengers in six different suites and gather them together in a spectacular captain's cabin that has a 180-degree view over the waves.

The comfort is enhanced by three living areas, by the privilege of a real projection room, a workout room at water level, a vast spa with *hammam*, sauna, and massage room—all the elements of a vacation complex recreated in an intimate setting and mixed with a gentle breeze of a breath coming from afar, where pleasure leaves its mooring.

Page 80
With its four bridges and its 246-foot
(75-m.) length, the *Ocean Victory* imposes
itself without difficulty as ruler of this
Caribbean bay. This is a prestigious
mooring for a yacht designed to sail
in the most beautiful waters of the world.

Left and facing page
Spaces where dining and conversation
commingle, others dedicated to tanning
and to relaxing, the different bridges of
the ship are used to form terraces in teak.
Treated according to an overriding
stylistic unity, they favor the natural,
and the simplicity of materials familiar
in the maritime universe. Produced
by Glyn Peter Machin, they are adapted
to the specific scale of the project.

Above

The interior and the exterior exist side by side
in harmony. The large bay windows that accentuate
the walls of the living room on the main bridge allow
one to appreciate the comfort on board. In the interior,
blue is the only color that stands out in an atmosphere
that favors soft earth tones. Its refinement comes
from the choice of woods, dominated by a waxed-look
oak, or by details such as the lines of inlay that outline
the design of the ensemble. The level of comfort
is striking, captured in the first glance at the low table
and the pouffes padded in leather.

Facing page
Providing better protection from
the daylight, the second living room
on the main bridge is closed off by
a large sculpture by Farhi in Plexiglas,
placed on a sideboard to break the
perspective. Blue remains the only
color used against the wood floors,
here treated in the manner of Versailles
parquet. A pair of antique deckchairs
in mahogany, placed at the entrance
to the living room, instills a subtle
confusion between the interior and
the exterior.

Right
Cabinet work is intimately linked to
the nautical world and this renovation
plays on all aspects of this art, as
shown in these details from a gaming
table, or the desk in plane and checker-
tree wood, with drawers livened up
by leather handles.

Above

The first living room that passengers encounter,
the main lounge is situated in the lower part of the ship.
Covered during the day, its purpose is to host
the receptions organized in the evenings. This large
room opens onto the formal dining room. As throughout
the yacht, the refinement is found in the details and
in the choice of materials that generate a warm
and natural atmosphere, heightened by the presence
of a few large paintings chosen to complement
the tones of the decor and to match the figurative
or abstract themes that evoke the maritime world.

Left and facing page
Above the paneling in light mahogany, the cornices are made with a piping of sycamore that livens the surface of the ceiling up to the central area; the effect is to enlarge the space of this cozy room. An attention to detail also reveals itself in the Indian-inspired embroidery of the cushions in jasper cotton, or in the fabric of the leather straps that cover the sofas and the armchairs. This material lends to the continuity of the sober and masculine atmosphere; it is also found, braided, around lamps, and as details at the bottom of blinds or on lampshades.

Above

At the level of the upper bridge, the dayroom opens mostly onto an outdoor dining area. It is symmetrically designed around a large braided wool rug of geometric design. Its design is by Alberto Pinto, as are the two tables in cracked lacquer, placed in front of large sofas that marry the curve of the design. These tables are notable in that they pivot to suit different configurations, and are adaptable to different kinds of uses.

Above

The back of the living room is decorated by two panels
in sky-blue shagreen on which a collection of plates
by Picasso is hung. At the center, the abstract
composition is by the artist Dominique Derive, based
on an idea by Alberto Pinto. It sections off an alcove
in which a bookcase with two console desks have
been placed. The detailed view of a low table created
by Alberto Pinto shows the button that allows one
to adjust its height into eight different positions.

Pages 96–97
The passageway that leads to the guest rooms is striking for its contrast of panels made of smooth and of braided wood, as well as the wavy handrail that is back-lit.

Facing page
This cabin is decorated in soft colors ranging from white to brown. The wall paneling is of braided sycamore and the furniture is veneered in reconstituted zebrawood. The adjoining bathroom presents a continuity of color in the jasper appearance of the stone.

Right
In one of the passageways, the walls are veneered in cabinetry panel whose design, created by Alberto Pinto, recalls the abstract nature of the sea floor. The console desk and the witch mirror are by Hervé van der Straeten. Each detailed view illustrates a search for refinement in the choice of material and the finesse of their craftsmanship.

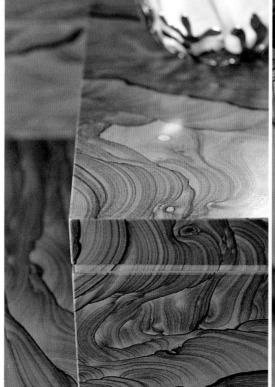

Above
The vast shipowner's cabin is located in the upper part
of the ship, in order to benefit from the 180 degree views.
It is modulated by blinds made of white wood slats.
It extends the vow of moderation and simplicity taken
for this yacht, with a decorative effect concentrating
on the linking of mahogany, plane, and sycamore woods,
reflected in the range of light-colored fabrics.
All the contours of the room are rendered functional
by a discreet continuity of storage spaces and of integrated
console desks.

Facing page

The shipowner's cabin is designed as a suite, with a corner living room, an area for dining, as well as a large bathroom and dressing room. From one room to another, the continuity of the design is assured by the use of the same woods and the details of the cabinetry, as in the blinds that enclose—with a bamboo effect— the white onyx of the vanity unit, or the shelf built around the edge of the cabin.

Right

Alberto Pinto likes to forge connections between materials, colors, and forms. This is shown in the chrome-tipped brace that he designed for the bench placed at the foot of the bed, repeated in the pouffe of the dressing room or in the embroidered motif created by Nicholas Chambeyron for Holland and Sherry, which enlivens the border of the bedspread and the edges of the cushions.

Left

The belly of the ship is given over to leisure; a movie theater has been created here, where twelve can relax on comfortable day beds. The walls and the ceiling are padded with acoustic fabric, ensuring that is it completely soundproof. Accessories such as reading lights integrated into the armrests have been specifically designed.

Facing page

The hammam opens out to a lighting display of a constellation of LEDs, which shows off the various finishes highlighted by the gray stone— polished, rough, or hammered. Water flows over a flooring of concentric layout in two tones of gray.

The Renovation of a Colonial House on a Small Caribbean Island

In entrusting the keys to an abandoned colonial inn to the decorator Alberto Pinto, its owner, a man of taste and of culture, knew that he was dealing with an individual who was more than capable of transforming the rough historicity of the place into a timeless fluidity.

Thanks to rediscovered techniques and multiple references, the old inn, situated on a Caribbean island, has retained its shell and not lost any of its antique charm. The interior, originally composed of a multitude of cramped cells, has been transformed. Woken up from a deep sleep passed in collective use, the spaces arch and reveal themselves around a garden-aquarium, an interior courtyard that extends an open living room and shares its freshness with the whole of the house.

The meeting of contrasts toward the emergence of a mixed unity constitutes the stylistic language of Alberto Pinto and plays a role in his seduction. Like a tango from Argentina, harmonically reworked to fit a contemporary rhythm, the colonial references are stripped of their rigid bitterness by inspired diversions. A wood ornament taken from a religious setting becomes a headboard, old linens are pieced together to form furniture coverings and curtains, a porcelain parrot engages in conversation with two ivory shellfish, and everywhere the poetry of the objects calls out to incite the emotion of surprise or sympathy.

A connoisseur of South America, Alberto Pinto subtly weaves the baroque exuberance and the earthly modesty that mark the features of this subcontinent. According to an assimilated and instinctive authenticity, he traces a personal line that echoes the clients' wishes.

The adventurous spirit of colonial times brings with it the eclecticism of resources composed not only of the Indo-Portuguese or Anglo-Indian confluences but also Brazilian and Hispanic. Plates from Rouen are juxtaposed with others from Savona, or imported by the East India Company, as a reminder of the centuries of trade between a virgin America and a conquering Europe.

Inhabited by the soul of time and vibrant with living and colorful references, the place is reborn as a serene reality, substituting the mercantile fever of the past with a search for simplicity and the sweetness of life.

The notion of relaxation during a vacation is underlined by a thread of cobalt blue which features throughout the renovation. Here, so close to the sea, there is no dining room, but rather a large kitchen where guests can gather in an informal way around an old table from a convent. The table reflects the image of this convivial house, which shares tranquility and comfort in a tropical setting on a picturesque island.

Page 106

The colonial inspiration for the interior
design can be seen straightaway
in the entrance hall by the eclectic choice
of objects from different lands.
The nineteenth-century rug is Portuguese,
as is the eighteenth-century console table.
Its baroque form is associated with a swan
in silver metal by Luis Ferreira, which draws
a line with the English mirror painted
in white. Around the mirror, the plates are
eighteenth century, coming from Rouen,
Savona, or imported from the East India
Company.

Left and facing page

A floor was sacrificed in order to free
up some space in this airy hall, which
is lit by natural light from the garden or,
once night falls, by a striking American
chandelier from the 1940s.

Pages 110–111
Under a frame covered in a veneer of braided bamboo, the conversion of the veranda creates a seamless link between the outside and the inside, with furniture made from petrified wood and sofas in rattan. The floor is parquet made from Ipê wood, one of the few woods from which such large boards can be made.

Facing page and right
Space is shared between a corner salon and a corner dining room. The decoration features mainly objects in ceramic, chosen for their resistance to humidity; notable is a collection of old Portuguese plates with the sea as their theme.

Pages 114–115
Linens are kept, arranged by color, in a rosewood cupboard, while crystal carafes fight for space in the china cabinet, which is decorated with bronze in the form of parrots, a favorite theme of this area, which opens out onto the garden.

Pages 116–117
In the middle of the large kitchen, the table, which comes from the refectory of an old convent, strikes a note of conviviality. The range hood is an architectural element, transformed and painted in white, like the walls. It comes from a local producer of decorative ceramics, other examples of whose work are placed on the table.

Left and facing page
The large living room basking in light is a natural extension of the veranda. Contrasts are thrown up by the Portuguese furniture in dark wood, the armchairs in varnished rattan, the ceiling lights in wrought iron, and a large screen in polychrome leather from Córdoba. Color comes through in motifs of embroidery in the form of red thread that embellishes the furnishings.

Pages 120–121
Two Dutch paintings from
the eighteenth century feature
a procession in the middle
of the composition. On the English
pedestal table, lobsters and crayfish
in ivory, like the fish in silver that
seem to swim up the wall, remind
us that we're not far from the beach.

Left and facing page
The decorator has faithfully conserved
the exterior appearance, maintaining
the illusion of doors leading to
bedrooms in this old country inn from
the seventeenth century. One could
never suspect from the outside
to what extent Alberto Pinto has
rethought the interior space, providing
a setting for rare and precious objects
of the kind that would have been brought
back from a voyage in colonial times.

Left and facing page
The corridor on the veranda leads
to three bedrooms in a row with a line
of royal blue that runs the length
of the white walls to outline the
contours of the house. In this room,
with an opening out into the garden,
the blue is linked to the red of the
handmade embroidery, and in the
natural spirit of the materials like
the straw rug, the braided rattan
of the armchairs, and of the lampshades
or the essences of the wood
on the inlaid screen. Around the bed,
the furniture links various epochs
and origins. The mirror is Venetian,
the desk with ivory handles is English,
the prie-dieu is French. On the walls,
the paintings are in oriental style.
Three traveling cases are piled high,
as if the owner is ready to leave for
a voyage.

Pages 126–127
The wood trellises painted in white define the space of this bathroom, decorated with an incredible English mirror, which provides a striking contrast in its dark wood frame sculpted with monsters and placed on the white marble of the counter top. It is hung on a wall covered with tiles made from designs by Alberto Pinto, by craftsmen who reproduced a motif from the eighteenth century for him.

Facing page and right
Against the windows that lead to the garden and a collection of rare orchids, a large chaise longue adds to the salon-type feeling that Alberto Pinto likes to give to the bathrooms he decorates. The perspective of this bathroom allows one to appreciate the large volume structured by the trellises.

Pages 130–131

A protruding paneled door, typical of Portuguese architecture, opens out into the blue room where a large herringbone rug is placed. The brass bed is English, produced in the nineteenth century. The covering of the four-poster bed is made up of old linens. The two Brazilian nightstands in Macassar wood hold bronze lamps in the form of parrots and Chinese porcelain candlesticks.

Left and facing page

The Brazilian desk is paired with a Portuguese chair; two matching chairs are placed on either side of the dresser, which is topped with three mandarins in porcelain. The bathroom adopts the same concept, but set in blue, as the red bedroom.

Facing page and right

The passageway on the second floor overlooks the grand entrance hall. The entryway receives additional light from the windows opening out onto the patio. It leads to two bedrooms that have been converted under the roof. From the wood guardrail painted blue, the complete openness of the space imposes itself in a generous and distinctive way. For this passageway, Alberto Pinto chose a pair of Portuguese banquettes from the eighteenth century in painted and gilded wood; two portraits are found in the medallions. On the ceiling, the two lanterns in etched glass are Indian in origin.

Pages 136–137
A view of the white room, situated in the gables of the house under the sloping roof. Its four-poster bed is adorned with a curtain in khadi, a very fine cotton woven by hand, which was then applied to a backing of a more durable fabric.

Left and facing page
The dark wood furniture contrasts with the sober and pristine atmosphere of the bedroom. The two Brazilian nightstands feature turned wood and have feet in the form of bear claws. They support a pair of brass lamps in the form of pineapples topped with lampshades of white sheet metal. The desk and the chair are both Portuguese. A series of English engravings depicting fish is hung on the walls.

Facing page
The second bedroom on this floor has also been designed in a pure white, giving contrast to the furniture, the artworks, and decorative objects, including the most unusual of them, an element of religious architecture transformed into a spectacular headboard. Two small oil paintings from Brazil, hung above the desk, depict two young nobles in their ceremonial clothes.

Right
The walls of the bathroom have a marble veneer, against which is contrasted a black wood dresser topped with a seashell and silver fishes. The silver-plated bathtub is an English model and dates from the nineteenth century. A plinth had to be specially made in order for it to be placed here.

A319: An Airplane in the Style of an English Club

In the imagination an airplane conjures up the idea of speed, of safety, and of escape. When it is limited to private use and decorated by Alberto Pinto, it incarnates the values of haute couture transported to the realm of decoration.

For this project—the conversion of an A319 for Acropolis Aviation—the decorator once again juggles with the codes of luxury and invents a cabin with all the allure of a select English club.

A series of three living spaces and a large bedroom with a bathroom make up this model of comfort for nineteen passengers. The capacity for commercial purposes is 120 people.

Stepping on to the plane, passengers are greeted by the caress of the leather and of the varnished wood that adorn the fulcrum of a large dressing area, leading to the view of the other rooms. This perspective is deepened by the special design of a carpet, whose geometric motif in two tones of beige carves out the space of the corridor. From one end to the other, the first living room encourages the free conversation of around ten people, who can take their seats either on a long sofa or in one of the various seats that recline according to preference. Retractable tables and low tables are just two of the elements that make life on board as much relaxation and diversion as work.

A large opening that doubles as a magazine rack leads to a second living area that transforms easily into a spacious dining room.

In fact, by the trick of an ingenious extension and the addition of two occasional seats, a dining table for eight people can appear, so that a gastronomic meal can be enjoyed in flight. The galley of the plane, arranged as a professional kitchen, allows cooking, from fresh ingredients, of any from the simplest to the most elaborate meals.

With its large double bed and its own bathroom with shower, the last cabin succeeds in making the plane's bedroom seem the size of a royal suite.

The nobility of the finishes and of the details support this feeling of exception, heightened by the very careful consideration given to the sources of lighting, which can change the atmosphere extremely precisely. High technology is certainly not neglected in this project. And yet, despite this, it's the quality of the stitching, the tension of the leather, or the finesse of the weaving which catch the eye, which becomes hopelessly seduced. The duality of the identical browns found in the leather and in the wood envelop the cashmere throws in a relaxing softness. It emanates from a warm feeling of relaxation by a fire.

Surpassing all standards, a flight aboard this aircraft places the moment of traveling in the rank of a voluptuous detour. At full speed, the space is sublimated and time is suspended.

Page 142

Varnished teak, soberly brought into focus by inserts
in polished nickel; the warmth of the various leathers
covering the armchairs, the cornice, or on the
decorative blinds; the decoration of the partitions
in beige suede; the cashmere of a blanket—each one
of these options contributes to the elegance of this
plane, in which the primacy of comfort communicates
with the luxury of the finishing touches.

Above

The perspective of the cabin allows one to appreciate
the great uniformity of the decorative scheme that
creates the atmosphere of an English club. The first
lounge becomes a comfortable living room with a very
large sofa covered in hand-woven velour, and a group
of three armchairs placed in a manner that suggests
a free and spontaneous configuration.

Left
Each element of detail illustrates
a search for perfection that expresses
itself in the choice of refined
techniques by the woodworker or
leather craftsman. They are brought
into focus by the subtle management
of lighting that multiplies the sources
of output in order to modulate its
intensity and play with the effects
of the fabrics—such as the braided
leathers, the inserts of metal in a wave
motif on the paneling, or the double
selvedge of the leather inserts that
decorate the blinds.

Facing page
A seat designed for crew members
shows as much concern for the
optimization of space as for the
aesthetic continuity seen throughout
the plane. Smooth gilded leather,
varnished teak—the materials and
finishes are identical to those in the
main cabin.

Facing page

As in the ensemble of wood fixtures in the plane, those of the corridor leading to the cabin are covered in several layers of varnish in order to create a brilliant effect, almost like a mirror. The dining room, thanks to an ingenious system of leaves and movable armchairs, allows up to eight diners to be seated around the large table.

Right

The entrance to the plane makes one think of a dressing room: an impression corroborated by its use, since it is here that the personal effects of the passengers are stored, which immediately conveys the measure of the conversion. The handles are imbued with the spirit of couture; the doors are covered in embossed and grooved leather. The design of the carpet was placed to complement the space.

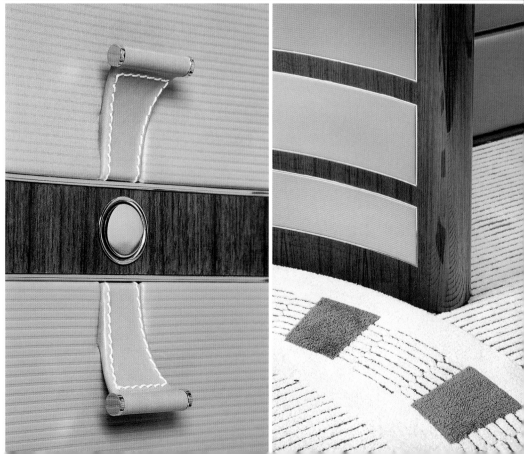

Left

Absolute luxury: the large bedroom is placed in the back of the plane. The frame of the bed is in teak and contains several drawers for storage, onto which is placed a king-size mattress, suggesting the most delectable comfort. The hand-tufted carpet extends the uniformity of the conversion, which differs here in the covering of the partitions and the lateral paneling, which is suede with a double selvedge, as well as in the choice of decorative blinds.

Above

Two small reading lamps in braided leather are placed on either side of the headboard. Embellished by a narrow nightstand veneered in varnished teak, the headboard benefits from easy access to the controls in polished nickel.

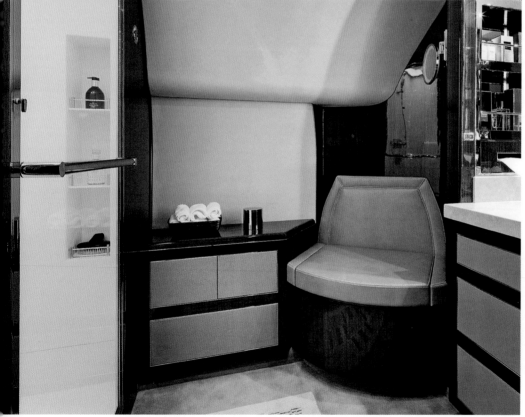

Left
Here, against gilded leather, bright nickel, and varnished teak, the principles of the conversion are carried through to the beautiful bathroom that elevates the room to the level of a true suite. It has the comfort of a large shower with a "rain" showerhead and overhead lighting. The sink in chrome is set into a marble countertop and the lavatory is in the form of a comfortable chair.

Facing page
Several cupboards are fitted in the bathroom, lending it the feel of a private dressing room. Here, as well, the carpet is in keeping with the overall unity of the conversion in a made-to-measure design. The bathroom linens match the bed linens designed for the plane.

Monaco: A Contemporary Duplex

In Monaco, in an old town house turned into a prestigious residence, Alberto Pinto is called on to decorate the contemporary interior of a large duplex. To this blank canvas he adds colors, within the constraint of a very short time frame and an imposed layout. Yet, in just three months, he managed to draw from this large area of 10,760 square feet (1,000 sq. m.) adjoining a 3,229 square feet (300 sq. m.) terrace, a decorative scenario that is highly individualized.

To achieve this, he coordinated—like an orchestral conductor—all the talents of the network of businesses and of artisans with which his studio collaborates. Guided by the desire for innovation that distinguishes his achievements, he mobilized his team to garner the spirit of great interior designers and create a large collection of exclusive furniture. The project also brought together 120 paintings, etchings, and screen prints. Sourced at the latest contemporary art fairs or in collaboration with the Maeght Gallery, they make up an artistic program consisting of sculptures and art objects to give the apartment a very geometric tone and a contemporary air.

Unable to alter the layout, the architect focused on volumes and spaces to offer a series of three modular rooms in the entrance of the apartment. Around the pivot of the first reception room, the row of volumes is punctuated by large arches that the sliding panels in bronze compartmentalize. In the last room, hidden behind a screen, the surprise of a dining room, decorated from wall to ceiling with a fresco by Dominique Derive, completes the space.

While this first level is designed to receive guests, the lower level is divided into various suites, introduced by a comfortable lounge onto which the main staircase opens. Each room, fitted with its own small *salon*, offers a particular setting that balances individual personality and personalization.

In this capital of the international jetset, where 128 different nationalities live side by side, the art of designing a pied-à-terre lies in the ability to seduce by distinctiveness without provocation. Alberto Pinto manages to infuse this charm by moving through harmonies of soft colors, awakened by some trenchant primary tones, as well as with the generous use of fine, appealing tactile and visual materials. He also captures the atmosphere of the good weather found in Monaco and the lightness of the sea air.

Combining plain lines in the service of an active social life, his decor reflects the spirit of the modern Riviera. The finished apartment represents a search for an ideal simplicity, as conducive to receiving people as to relaxation, a home whose ultimate luxury is to be open and accessible to all.

Page 154
The high standard of the solutions
implemented in record time in this
apartment conversion is striking.
It is seen in the treatment of doors,
made in the manner of decorative
panels, and in the rug, woven after
an original design by Alberto Pinto.

Left and facing page
The various rooms on the reception
floor are separated by sliding doors
that were designed as marquetries
in bronze set in different patinas
applied in a cold process. This effect
allows the highlighting of the
juxtaposition of the pieces that are as
much sculptures as furniture, as well
as an important hanging of lithographs
and contemporary artworks.

Pages 158–159
The large painting by Ralph Fleck underlines the capacity of Alberto Pinto to coordinate pieces of original furniture and a large number of artworks according to a scheme that is at once selective and coherent.

Facing page and right
The series of adjoining living rooms opens out onto a terrace of 3,229 square feet (300 sq. m.), furnished with pieces in bleached wood. They are designed to be multipurpose, thanks to the large sliding doors that open out to unify the spaces. At the heart of this living room is a small dining table: the low table was created by Alberto Pinto, who plays on the different finishes of the bronze and on the textures of the glass.

Pages 162–163

The transition between the living room and the dining room was conceived to spectacular effect. It manages to hide—until the last moment—the surprise of the table placed behind the panels of a screen, a golden surface on which graceful goldfish swim. This tribute to art deco mingles with the inspiration of the contemporary, with a large fresco by Dominique Derive. This covers the walls and the ceiling of a dining room that can host ten diners around a large, circular table.

Facing page and right

In the service corridor, a light console holds a sculpture by the artist Machat, who created many of the works that adorn the apartment. The large screen that separates the living room and the dining room is decorated in a different theme on each of its sides. On the side shown, it presents the silver sheen of moonlight on a background of black lacquer.

Left and facing page

The lower level of the apartment is a more private space from which the various suites emanate. They are introduced by a large, luminous living room, punctuated by touches of red and of blue that are dispersed on the rug of original design and on the re-embroidered cushions and in the lithographs of Mirò, Aki Kuroda, and Marco del Re. The guardrail of the wrought-iron staircase was produced from a drawing by Alberto Pinto. It creates a graphic impetus and imparts a dynamism that is underlined by a colored group of sculptures by Malevitch, placed in front of the understairs cupboard. In the hallway, two works of photography by Sergio Giral Jr face each other.

Facing page and right

The third living room on the reception floor has been turned into a television room. On an occasional table whose bush-hammered wooden feet evoke a totem sculpture by Brancusi, a sculptured lamp diffuses a soft light that gives life to the different patinas of the bronze door.

Pages 170–171

In the continuity of the room brought together by a very large rug, a living room is converted by composite furniture that associates, among other things, deep low chairs with an outdoor spirit, or perhaps a pouffe by Hervé van der Staeten with patent leather armchairs. On the walls, lithographs by Takis, Calder, and Braque are hung. The lacquered screen opens out onto the dressing room.

Left and above:
Each one of the bedrooms follows a different plan that plays
on the colors and the attributes of several important pieces.
In one of them, a canopy bed found in an Italian designer's shop
gives structure to the space. In another, a large screen in gilded
wood, drawn and made to the specifications set out by Alberto Pinto,
segments the room.

Alfa Nero: A Theater on the Waves

Celebrated as a model ship, awarded prizes around the world by the most informed juries, the *Alfa Nero*, a spectacular 272-feet (83-m.) yacht built by Oceanco, made the headlines in 2007 at the time of its launch. Today, many still follow its trail and witness the magical attraction of this sleek ship.

With its black hull, shiny as onyx, a huge rear deck equipped with an infinity pool, and a dynamic and sporty look, this boat is not one to go unnoticed.

Dedicated to leisure and receptions, the *Alfa Nero* has the look from the outside like an amphitheater rising above the spectacle of the waves; Alberto Pinto designed a conversion in line with the silhouette of the ship, playing on the strong symmetry and contrast of black and white.

A tone of elegance is set, which permeates and develops throughout the ship in the decoration; the ocean lends the shimmer of its changing reflections and patterns. They are offered through a rich palette of materials: many types of wood, leather, shagreen, parchment, and cotton cloth with fine embroidery, as well as innovative solutions such as dappled lacquer panels, or inlays of etched glass blocks.

This kind of luxury—inherited from the great tradition of yachting and of ocean liners—surfaces on the gentle wave in tribute to art deco. The freedom of style is linked to jazz and modernity: Alberto Pinto likes to grab these references to create a series of sparkling and warm atmospheres, somewhere between the worlds of *The Great Gatsby* and the Roaring Twenties. The brilliant ambience that embraces the main deck, which is exposed to daylight and therefore preferred in the evenings. A box of polished wood, its depth is enhanced by the straight lines of its two parquet floors in tones of light and dark wood. Dining and living rooms follow one another up to the music room, where a grand piano signed Marco Del Re for Pleyel invites guests to gather around for joyful improvisations.

Surrounded by a staircase in leather and ebony, an elevator leads to the bright white rooms of the upper deck, favored during the day, where—set half outside—the circle of a dining room opens into the distance.

Several suites and cabins have been designed to accommodate a dozen passengers. An echo of the world of travel and of boating, each suite is unique in that a dominant color evokes the enveloping gentleness chosen to accompany the time of relaxation.

At once graphic and yet imbued with a soft luxury, *Alfa Nero* elevates the concept of pleasure to a rare level of achievement, pleasure that has been taken on a new course by Alberto Pinto.

Pages 174–175
The *Alfa Nero's* upper deck is a balcony overlooking the sea. Symmetrically flanking the window of a skydome are two large sofas upholstered in white cotton fabric underscored by fringed black trimming.

Left and facing page
The lower deck is arranged as a large reception space that turns into a nightclub in the evening. Parallel bands of two-tone wood flooring extend the perspective as sitting rooms and dining alcoves follow one another. Opposite a Roy Lichtenstein painting is a piano designed by Marco Del Re for Pleyel. The walls are enlivened by different varieties of wood with panels of glass and parchment that create a plush atmosphere.

Left

A Bijou coffee table is set in the middle of the music room. The large sofas are upholstered in two tones of chenille fabric, both picked up in the appliqué cushions. The carpet was designed by Alberto Pinto in an outsized cross-stitch embroidery pattern.
The stairway walls are lined in leather, as are the steps which include strips of Macassar ebony. The back-lit niche features a sculpture by Farhi. Sycamore is another variety of wood favored on this deck.

Right

The dining service is stored in its own custom cupboard to protect it from rolling seas.

Left
The leisure-oriented *Alfa Nero* boasts
a retractable pontoon that provides
direct access to the sea from
a "beach club" decorated with two Roy
Lichtenstein paintings. In this same
holiday spirit, the outer decks extend
across surfaces unusual even for this
type of craft. They are systematically
furnished in the black-and-white motif
that characterizes the ship's hull.

Facing page
Fully 60 percent of the dining room
can be opened onto the exterior.
It also features radial parquet flooring
of sycamore enhanced by shiny
metal inserts. The chandelier was
designed in conjunction with Ozone.
In the adjoining sitting room,
the textured lacquer panels are framed
by Macassar ebony.

Facing page

The orange cabin boasts a double bed, unlike the other two. The office of the ship owner's suite gives an idea of the master's private domain. It features louro-faia wood cornices, bookshelves, and desk, with a complementary variety of wood on the parquet floor. The large metallic door panels were executed from Pinto's designs.

Right

Three cabins are furnished along a similar design conjugated in three different colors. Leather and canvas appliqués evoke the spirit of travel, as does a selection of photos on shell themes by Vincent Leray.

Left
Two matching suites present the same concept in different hues—coral and turquoise—with embroidery and print motifs inspired by branching coral and algae. This theme recurs in wall lights designed by Hervé van der Straeten specially for the ship, set against paneling in a weave of three varieties of wood, on which also hang shell photos by Vincent Leray. The armchairs in the sitting alcoves date from the 1940s.

Facing page
The bathrooms in these suites extend the decorative motif via a floor carpeted with three types of marble and cupboards veneered with a weave of woods.

Kuwait City: An Orientalist Palace

Growing up around the pearl trade that flourished on its shores, forging a link between caravans and ships, Kuwait City has—since the eighteenth century—traded with both East and West.

On the seafront of this port city, a family home reflects centuries of travel, shimmering its patina sheen of dawn and of dusk. Its decor evokes the authenticity of traditional architectural styles, diverted toward the invention of solutions in which all facets of the Islamic East sparkle.

A monumental opening on the nave, transformed from a mosque in Egypt; a detour to Rajasthan in a ceremonial dining room; resurgent Ottoman elements for the master of the house; Persian themes for the girl's room: each step in this palace imperceptibly crosses borders marked by the presence of an artwork or an object d'art, antique furniture, of a color or of a particular technique.

Space and light are modeled through an expertise maintained and improved on by a network of selected artisans from France, Morocco, or Egypt. Carpets of marble, gilt, and mirrors whisper in the light, dimmed by some proficient sleight of hand, while finely carved plasterwork, panels of carved wood or of marquetry, stencils, and embossed leather from Córdoba combine architecture and decor.

Master of a heightened orientalism, Alberto Pinto reveals a wide panorama of influences, combined in a magical and lively light. Thanks to the memorable days of childhood spent in Casablanca, he has, written onto his soul, the mysteries of this subtle and brilliant *art de vivre*, which he projects with simple timelessness. It forms the echo of an erudite setting, a connection of spirit forged between generations for a thousand and one lives.

The posterity that one wishes for a family home is expressed in this way of presenting the history of the forms, in interpreting it by the colors of the century. There is not a reference that is not revisited. To give one example among many others: the old Prelle fabrics used to cover chairs and sofas in the spacious living room are woven with a blue turquoise thread specially chosen by Alberto Pinto, to appeal to the superstitious nature of the lady of the house.

Above all, Alberto Pinto likes to introduce these recognizable elements that allow his clients to appropriate the place with alacrity, to distill the surprise and astonishment, while promoting the benchmarks established by the paintings of masters and of antiques brought from a previous house. As when painting a portrait, in which the subject has to recognize itself, but also to discover itself, the family have—driven by Alberto Pinto—discovered a new light, and opened a new chapter in their lives.

Page 186
Architecture and decor mix intimately
in this house that fuses many inspirations
and techniques of the Orient. The motifs
under the arches are borrowed from
a Syrian palace and the marble
foundation from a Cairo mosque.

Left and above
The monumental entrance appears under
an elevated nave, two floors from ground
level. Its chandelier is a creation derived
from a piece found at an antique shop
in Alexandria, reproduced here in a much
larger size by Stefan Mocanu for Alberto
Pinto. Each of its glass globes was
blown in Bohemia. In a niche of the
galleries ornamented with antiques,
a Portuguese medal from the eighteenth
century is topped by two chandeliers
from Europe dating from the nineteenth
century.

Left

The carpet of marble on the floor, with its central fountain, is inspired by a palace in Cairo. Its colors are diffused in the columns and the arches stenciled by Laurent Beuffe, who has succeeded masterfully in giving an ancient look to his work. The door panels are masterpieces of inlaid tortoiseshell on a gold, pearl, and lemon tree background; a subtle technique that comes in handy when it comes to covering the air-conditioning unit in a lace of gypsum. The choice of artworks underlines the same refinement, with, placed above the tip of an incense burner, a very rare model of an eighteenth-century mosque.

Facing page

A very beautiful collection of oriental paintings and antiques adorns the sides of the entrance hall.

Left
With its marble floor, the dining room
is an enchantment of mirrors and
of gilding covering the wood, bronze,
and resin motifs that trace blooming
foliage on the walls. The large table
can seat eighteen guests, who eat
together under coffered ceilings
inspired by an Ottoman palace
in Istanbul.

Facing page
The stunning effect of the walls,
inspired by a palace in Rajasthan,
is enhanced by the embedding
of small Indian mirrors, as well as fine
points of gold. The technique of
embroidery used to adorn the backs
of chairs involves gold thread in
an Ottoman tradition. The chandeliers
are Alberto Pinto creations.

Pages 194–195
The panels, columns, and trellises
of the grand salon are in carved oak,
evoking in the wood the mosque in
Granada. Nowadays this inspires
alcoves with a more secular use,
displaying works of art like the painting
by Pasini at the center of the image.

Left and facing page
Discreet touches in turquoise blue
punctuate the entire decor, including
two armchairs upholstered in an
antique Prelle fabric, re-embroidered
in the color found in the curtains.
The color illuminates the amber
atmosphere, to which the great
chandelier in Indian crystal contributes.
Bone inlays on the ledges bear
the calligraphy of lines of poetry.

Facing page

At the entrance hall, a powder room diffuses glints of silver. The sink unit is covered in nacre—an inspiration from Mexico; covering its pilasters and bases is glass, painted using a Spanish technique and dominated by mukarnas topped in silver.

Right

The antechamber to the householder's apartments: an alcove allows one to wait on a comfortable couch, which is covered with a variety of cushions embroidered with Fez petit point. The pattern is repeated in stencil on the woodwork, background to a painting by George Willoughby-Maynard. The large censer in the center of the marble floor is an eighteenth-century Syrian model; the chandelier and the lamp come from mosques.

Pages 200–201
Typically Arabic, the living room of the householder's apartments reveals embroidered couches put against walls to free the central area, which is filled by a large Persian rug. The decorative plan focuses on the coffered ceiling and a collection of ancient calligraphy enhanced by the stenciled walls.

Facing page
The ceiling of the dining room is decorated with woodwork painted using a Moroccan technique. Mashrabiyas of oak and walnut decorate the walls. They are carved with geometric patterns from Asia Minor that let in natural light or reflect it by the use of mirrors.

Right
The antique crystal chandelier was purchased in Istanbul in order to complement a set of pieces of gilded crystal of Indian origin, distinctively is that they are enhanced by an interior of green enamel.

Left

The desk lends a Moorish touch, also suggested by the architecture of the wooden cornices and the Cordovan leather applied to the walls. The desk is reconstituted from a piece of palace furniture. Facing it is a small table made entirely of tortoiseshell. Valuable elements, such as the Bohemian crystal cups that can be seen on the Macassar ebony and satinwood table, are made according to a Spanish model. Above the bookcases, Turkish tiles are displayed.

Above

The panels of the doors have been crafted in an Egyptian workshop that perpetuates the art of cabinetmaking, using bone, tortoiseshell, and satinwood.

Pages 206–207
The family room is decorated in a
modern eclectic style, highlighted by
touches of coral color. These are found
on the couches and embroidered
cushions, on rugs inspired by the 1930s,
and on the ceiling—which mimics that
of a floating palace on the Bosphorus—
or the chandeliers, contemporary
replicas of an antique model fitted
with oil lamps.

Facing page and above
The calligraphy of an order for a mission
originally sent by a sultan hangs above
a Mazarin desk in inlaid wood. On the
lacquered gaming table, spikes from
standards are turned into decorative
objects. Around the dining area,
Hispano-Moorish ceramics are placed
on wooden ledges.

Left

A young girl's room is inspired by
fifteenth-century Persian miniatures
representing ceremonial tents.
Two different techniques are applied
to the fabric covering the walls
to replicate the effects suggested
by these old documents. They are
both painted and re-embroidered
to give more strength to the decor.

Facing page

An adjoining small room off the
bedroom is composed around
a nineteenth-century papier-mâché
table. The sofa is covered in Indian
silk and flanked by two Anglo-Indian
pedestals. On the walls hang two
Persian gouaches. The headboard
adopts the pointed arch characteristic
of Oriental architecture. Both bedside
tables are of palm wood.

Facing page
Corridors crisscross under a skylight
carved from niches into which antique
ceramics are placed. Their colors stand
out from the pristine white walls and
carved plaster and reflect those of the
marble floor. In the center, the table
holds a ceramic piece, mounted like
a mosque lamp.

Right
The living room of the main suite is
topped by a cornice of oak punctuated
with bas-reliefs of pierced bone.
Its furniture includes a large side
cabinet in baroque style, and a Spanish
nineteenth-century piece in ebony
and rosewood, inlaid with tortoiseshell
and mother-of-pearl. The vignette
on the left shows bathroom furniture
inspired by the royal palace in Cairo.

Left

The master bedroom opens onto a
large terrace plunging down to the sea.
It is decorated with a sky-blue tapestry
on top of which are decorations
in laced oak inspired by the Alhambra.
Cornices are punctuated by pierced
circles of bone. The headboard is
made from an Ottoman model, while
the embroidered bedspreads are from
a drawing in the oriental-inspired
fashion, made for Marie-Antoinette
in the eighteenth century.

Facing page

The door panels inlaid with bone,
mother of pearl, oyster shell, and
ebony open onto the living room,
giving a view from which we can see
a painting by Johann Victor Krämer,
representing a scene of instruction
in a Koranic school in the nineteenth
century.

Facing page and right
The bathroom for the lady of the house plays with shimmering mirrors, etched and aged, arranged around a large mirror from Murano covering the vanities. This room is separated from the dressing room with a boudoir lined with blue hangings embroidered with diamond shapes. It is lit by a glass chandelier reproduced from a model of the 1930s; the same design is also found in the dressing room.

Pages 218–219
The dressing room used by the man of the house resembles a ship's cabin. Its walls, covered in wood paneling, are enlivened by mother-of-pearl and tortoiseshell, with crescent moon motifs—they are a Turkish inspiration. The nineteenth-century English armchair has retained the charm of its patina.

Gulfstream 550: A Jewel of an Airplane

Backdrop to a nomadic lifestyle, a link between various properties scattered throughout the world, this Gulfstream 550 is the ultimate extension of the private domain of a Brazilian client of Alberto Pinto's.

Expert in the conversion of private planes, the fact that his studio was able to complete the project in just one year, from the light beige of the fuselage to the implementation of the cabin, is witness to a search for absolute customization.

Capable of carrying eighteen passengers, the jet is divided into a spacious front cabin, organized by various combinations of armchairs and sofas, and an aft cabin consisting of two facing sofas that convert to become a double bed and transform the space into a bedroom. With an interior plan only thirteen meters by just over two (approximately 43 x 7 feet), ingenuity and versatile solutions were needed. In this regard, an adjustable table was developed: a table for four diners in its upper position; a piece of furniture more in keeping with the atmosphere of a living room in its lower position.

The size of the decor puts paid to any sense of confinement. The luxurious essentiality of quality materials, treated with sophistication, brings warmth and avoids monotony. On the partitions and furniture, a veneer of polished rosewood dominates, chosen in this version to obtain a homogeneous grain that adds a graphic momentum to the composition, while evoking the sheen of straw marquetry in ebony on the shelves.

Leather also holds a place of honor. Shagreen on the foundations, the leather is a light velvety suede around the windows, following the line of the oval and adorning it with large, diamond-stitches. On the front of the chairs, it is smooth and tan, enhanced with brown piping, echoing the color of the lapel and braided sides.

This duality of color, which is repeated on the carpet with a made-to-measure design, responds to the request of the client, who wanted to reproduce the look of one of her husband's favorite ties. Inspired by a checkerboard, a light background is animated by the reproduction in color of the random, lozenge-shaped pattern, solid or hollow, in brown or beige.

Satin, delicately gilded to avoid any ostentatiousness, completes the subtle scheme by highlighting the control units of the armchairs, by identifying the lighting, and by digging into the thin threads of the woodwork.

A jewel of an airplane, decorated with a feminine touch, this design triumphs thanks to the finest expertise. Often ignored by developers of aircraft, this know-how is what is asked of Alberto Pinto's studio; he goes beyond the available skills of each trade to achieve the highest degree of perfection.

Page 220
This conversion shows ranges from beige to dark brown. The wood chosen for the cabinetwork is Indian teak, which is known for its very uniform fiber.

Pages 222–223
The carpet that unifies the entire cabin is made of hand-tufted wool. In the diamond-shape motifs, it takes up the dominant colors of the conversion, dividing this part of the plane into a club, a living room composed of a couch facing two chairs, and a corner dining room.

Facing page and right
The chairs are upholstered in gilded leather highlighted in dark piping; their arms and backs are upholstered in coffee-colored woven leather. The walls are covered with straw-colored suede and the side paneling is in shagreen leather. The levers are made of satinized copper.

Above

The table of the corner dining area folds down its wings into the position of a low table. Satinized copper inserts, placed in contrast to the black wood, highlight the attractiveness of the Indian teak.

Right

The table set for two allows one to appreciate the precious and soberly feminine atmosphere given to this unit designed for a Brazilian client by Alberto Pinto. It is exclusively for her that he chose this combination of refined materials and of finishes, making this plane a true jewel. A second cabin extends this idea, with two sofas facing each other that can unfold to form a bed on which to rest during long flights.

A Contemporary Orientalism in Kuwait City

In Kuwait City, Alberto Pinto writes—for a young man—a new page in the history of oriental style. With fine continuity, he directs it toward a simple reading, rhythmic and masculine, which allows him to highlight a large collection of works and objets d'art collected by the master of the house. An eclectic group, whose inspirations converge in the realization of the layout and decor.

This synthesis catches the eye from the stairs leading to the apartments; it expresses the spirit of the organization as a whole: namely, the search for an emphasis on the works, on which the ascent offers a multitude of points of view.

The contrast of black and white sets the tone here as well, in various shades between the metal of the ramp, the dark wood of the handrail, the Baccarat chandelier, the marble floor, and immaculate stucco walls. A touch of red from an avant-garde painting boosts the contrast, which serves as a link between a purely contemporary inspiration and resurgences of the spirit of the 1900s, embodied by a beautiful set of furniture by Carlo Bugatti, whose architectural element, like an opening signal of his style, is hung in the staircase.

The shift to postmodernity culminates in the grand salon, where contemporary Middle Eastern art shows its creativity and liveliness of imagination. Around these works, the furniture is designer and traditional techniques are updated, sometimes in a roundabout way, to serve the graphic momentum of black and white.

The ceiling transposes the motif from a palace in Turkey, there painted in several colors, into the blackened oak moldings that come off a limed oak trim. The arabesque is subtly reflected in veneers of ebony inlaid with bone, which highlight the frames on the walls or on the bookcases. From their base, plates of bone reveal meticulous landscapes painted in ink. On the parquet floor of blackened wengé, white armchairs and sofas stand out, as does the use of stainless steel.

In the large office, the link to the past stretches even further, without distorting the main theme of a clean contrast.

The furniture by Carlo Bugatti, precious constructions that celebrate the intelligence of the hand, invite reminiscences of the 1930s as well as of the resources of a traditional ornamental heritage. It is an atmosphere in which paintings by masters of the nineteenth-century orientalists exalt a nobility torn from history.

The adjoining bathroom fuses the present with the timeless. Carved in Carrara marble, it channels light and leads to a pure, contemporary abstraction, highlighting furniture reduced to a minimum in a counterpoint of black lacquer, a frieze of stylized Kufic calligraphy, and an alabaster chandelier from 1930.

Page 228
In the bedroom of this grand apartment, treated with a contemporary orientalist approach, part of the collection of furniture by Carlo Bugatti is placed, including a small table positioned under the portrait of a sage.

Above and right
In the living room, the contrast of black and white is used as a driving force for the decor, and set off by touches of bright red, as in the grand staircase where the color is added by a contemporary work that illustrates the mix of influences of this conversion. The stair railing in wrought iron and wood is reproduced from the model of a town house. The chandelier is Baccarat, the hung architectural element by Bugatti.

Facing page
On a living-room wall, a large canvas
evokes the tradition of calligraphy
through contemporary conventions.
It is hung above a sculptural piece of
furniture whose body is in fact chrome.
Playful and sweet at the same time,
a sculpture of the iconic Birkin bag by
Hermès, cast in stone, takes its place.
The low table was created by Alberto
Pinto, the blackened wood base set
on spheres of chrome metal. The side
table is a model by Baker in a special
chrome finish.

Right
A Hervé van der Straeten chandelier
is suspended from the ceiling of limed
oak, whose blackened bas-reliefs
repeat the pattern—which was
originally polychrome—from a Turkish
house. The staircase is placed under
a partitioned skylight.

Left

Around the fireplace lined with decorative candles, white sofas and easy chairs are set off chromatically from the blackened wengé parquet chosen for the entire apartment. Between the two red lamps with thorny bodies, the exploded zither is a work by Arman. On the low table, the small black crystal horse is a Baccarat creation.

Above

The border is made of ebony wood paneling inlaid with bone. At the foot of the bookcase, the panels illustrate various scenes that reference aspects of the Kuwaiti world, drawn in ink on plates of bone. They illustrate the link between tradition and modernity, maintained throughout the decorative scheme, which is at the same time very contemporary.

Above

The walls of the room accommodate
the hanging of orientalist paintings.
They stand out from white walls
with pilasters in carved gypsum.
The contemporary chandelier, created
by designer Kevin Reilly, lights up the
collection of furniture by Carlo Bugatti,
brought together by the owner, a man
inspired by the "1900 spirit" of the
master and also strongly influenced
by the techniques of oriental crafts.

Facing page

A small secretary by Carlo Bugatti is
used as a bedside table on which a lamp
in white parchment is placed.
The headboard is framed by tiles
of etched mirrors. On the cushions,
Brandenburg embroidery picks up
the contrast of black and white.

Left
The Royère inspired lampshade puts into perspective the subtlety of the incisions made in the plaster by Moroccan craftsmen, specialists in this traditional art, and break the linearity of the white walls. At the foot of the bed, on which the bedspread is tied with Brandenburg trimmings, stands an Indian bench in ebony inlaid with bone.

Facing page
Facing daylight, the desk and chair are works by Carlo Bugatti. The bathroom stretches out in the purified atmosphere of a hammam; the decorative scheme creates a contrast with a gray-veined white marble background highlighted by a black marble vanity unit and an inscription in stylized Kufi. The alabaster chandelier is a French creation from the 1930s.

HRO Défense Ouest:
A Corporate Conversion on a Human Scale

A daily destination, an office building is a part of everyday life. This obvious fact guides Alberto Pinto in the realization of his corporate projects. Pioneer in this area, he was one of the first important decorators to humanize these vast spaces, which were in the past delivered empty and disembodied.

The emergence of this practice, in a profession all too often rapidly circumscribed to the domain of large houses, could seem incongruous. And yet, in the same vein as the decoration of ships and airplanes, the investment of Alberto Pinto in business sectors extends his capacity to respond instinctively to the requirement of his clients.

One of those who brought him here, almost thirty years ago, to be the master of the genre, was Howard P. Ronson, founder of the HRO group, and among the most important developers of office buildings in Europe and the United States.

First as a client for his private houses, then for his own office space, Howard Ronson was won over by the ease with which Alberto Pinto knew how to satisfy his desires; he asked him to apply the science of staging and decoration to the buildings constructed by his company. In the early 1980s this was a novel idea that immediately seduced the decorator, naturally inspired by the grand dimensions.

Those that have been entrusted to him since then have been gigantic, as in the 624,306 square feet (58,000 sq. m.) of the HRO Défense Ouest, a complex for which he supervised the conversion and layout of the 161,458 square feet (15,000 sq. m.) garden, designed with Eric Ciborowski. Above all, he imagined the group of communal spaces and service areas, including five large lobbies, a large auditorium, several multipurpose rooms, a cafeteria, a gym, two restaurants serving 2,400 meals daily, as well as a group of vertical and horizontal corridors.

Alberto Pinto is in his element in these grand proportions, defying standardization and anonymity. With the help of quality materials, with innovative solutions and original works, he qualifies each sequence of space. With a cinematographic enthusiasm, he sees the corridors as long animated scenes, all the while accentuating the horizontal elements of the architecture in order to guarantee the breadth of an enlarged field of vision.

Rhythm, art, and oversized dimensions make up the theatrical elements in the lobbies. High points in the project, they are different but also held together in the same spirit, in order to give structure to the prestigious interfaces between the facades in the clear glass wall-curtain, polished concrete and stone, and the interior of the building.

In the extension of the largest business district in Europe, HRO Défense Ouest affirms itself by this unusual decorative program. A quality of image that from the outset seduces prestigious companies, concerned to invest in places that reflect dynamism and notoriety.

Page 240
The entrance hall opens onto the vast atrium of the office complex, HRO Défense Ouest, whose gardens were designed by Eric Ciborowski. Its monumental space is soberly furnished with two waiting rooms delineated by a circular carpet of original design, with two large Toro armchairs from Azucena and a table by designer Eric Schmitt.

Left and facing page
The three secondary entrance halls each have as their own centerpiece a chandelier by Ingo Maurer and a monumental sculpture by Sophia Vari, whose color is a reference, picked up again on the large marble reception desk, protected by a glass box, which was also designed by the sculptor.

Pages 244–245
In the third secondary hall, frosted glass is replaced by staff imitating metal frames. The large banquette was created by designer Jean-Marie Massaud for Cappellini.

Left and facing page
The elevators continue the decorative scheme of the halls. A waiting room is decorated in light oak veneer with borders of dark oak. It serves as a meeting room that converts into a dining room. The walls are of the same wood veneer, radiating on panels stitched with large leather laces, and decorated with original watercolors by Roger van Rogger, by a portrait of the artist, and by reproductions of sconces by Pierre Chareau.

Facing page
In the foyer of the auditorium lies a large ocher carpet, at the end of which is placed a banquette by Jean-Marie Massaud, under a bas-relief by Lenka Beillevert. The hanging of architectural photographs by Ludovic Alussi, taken in the business district of La Défense in Paris, creates an effect of abyss. They are underlined, and thus highlighted, by console tables.

Right
Two thousand people eat lunch every day in the 10,760 square feet (1,000 sq. m.) set aside for the restaurant developed by Alberto Pinto. The complex also features a bar and a club separated by custom-made black lacquer screens by Philippe Hurel. The whole is unified by blue stucco walls and large panoramic photographs on the theme of water.

Pages 250–251
A large roll runs the entire length and height of the main lobby like a sheet of parchment. The monumental chandelier was made to order for Alberto Pinto by the artist Stefan Mocanu, like the two metal wall-lighting fixtures topped with resin pellets, which are found on a smaller scale in other areas of the conversion.

Facing page and right
The two-hundred-seat auditorium is lined with faux leather acoustic panels, punctuated by Eagle wall-lighting fixtures by Lumen Italia. The back stage is composed of a puzzle of light oak panels laid on a dark oak base to form a geometric composition.

The showroom

In 2011, Alberto Pinto opened a new showroom of 807 square feet (75 sq. m.) on rue du Mail in Paris. Open by appointment only, he presents pieces in limited editions that receive the stamp "Pinto Paris," a brand launched in 2010 by the designer to diffuse to a wider public some of the furniture and accessories specifically designed for his projects.

Made with the help of master craftsmen and -women with whom the designer is used to working, each object reflects excellent craftsmanship and the application of sophisticated techniques. They also show Alberto Pinto's preference for associating raw materials with those of quality, or contrasting different kinds of finishes.

Two collections have been launched to date. The first, Rio, is a tribute to the seductive qualities of the materials and colors of Brazil. The second, called Vulcain, showcases Alberto Pinto's researches into sculptural furniture, as shown in the Chaos console table illustrated on the facing page. Shown in an ambience of a cozy apartment, alternating living room and dining room, these collections show the timeless lines that renew the heritage of the great interior designers. An underlying consistency is offset by the identity given to each piece, designed to exist independently or in dialogue with works of art and objects, as here with a tapestry by Calder, or feather headdresses from South America.

Author

Julien Morel developed an interest in contemporary art while studying art history at the École du Louvre. He began his career in communications as a writer for a public relations firm specializing in lifestyle and design, where he was introduced to distinguished designers such as Alberto Pinto. He also wrote *Alberto Pinto: Today*, published in 2010 by Flammarion.

Acknowledgements

Maison Alberto Pinto thanks the Oceanco and Feadship dockyards for their kind collaboration. Julien Morel warmly thanks Benoît Chottin and the entire team at Maison Alberto Pinto who enlightened him about the manifold intricacies of these magnificent sites. Thanks also to Laurent d'Estrées and Aurélia Maillard for their valuable support.

Maison Alberto Pinto

Show room Pinto Paris
11, rue d'Aboukir – 75002 Paris
Tel.: +33 (0)1 40 13 00 00
Fax: +33 (0)1 40 13 75 80
www.pintoparis.com – www.albertopinto.com

Additional Alberto Pinto Titles
Alberto Pinto *Classics*
Alberto Pinto *Moderns*
Alberto Pinto *Orientalism*
Alberto Pinto *Corporate*
Alberto Pinto *Table Settings*
Alberto Pinto *Today*

Editorial Director: Ghislaine Bavoillot
Translated from the French by Orhan Memed
Design: Isabelle Ducat
Copyediting: Penny Isaac
Typesetting: Claude-Olivier Four
Proofreading: Helen Woodhall
Color Separation: Reproscan, Bergamo, Italy
Printed in Italy by Grafiche Flaminia

Simultaneously published in French
as *Alberto Pinto: Autour du monde*
© Flammarion, S.A., Paris, 2011

English-language edition
© Flammarion, S.A., Paris, 2011

editions.flammarion.com

12 13 14   4 3 2

ISBN: 978-2-08-020093-8

Dépôt légal: 11/2011

Photographic credits
Jacques Pépion: pp. 2–3; 4; 8–13; 14–43; 44–65; 106–141; 154–173; 186–219; 220–227; 228–239; 240–253; 254–255
Vanessa Von Zitzewitz: p. 6
Luc Boegly: pp. 66–79; 142–153
Courtesy of Oceanco–Pamela Jones: pp. 174–185 / www.oceancoyacht.com
Courtesy of Feadship: pp. 80–105 / www.feadship.nl

Credits
Front cover, pp. 14, 17: *Guéridon* © Claude Lalanne / ADAGP, Paris 2011
Back cover, p. 167: © Kasimir Malevitch
pp. 2, 156, 157, 159: *Aillebeu 17/Il Titieu* © Ralph Fleck / ADAGP, Paris 2011
pp. 2, 162, 165: © Dominique Derive
pp. 3, 157: © Dominique Mercy / ADAGP, Paris 2011
pp. 4, 16, 17: © Marc Quinn
p. 8: © Isabelle Magor
p. 8: © Christian Bérard / ADAGP, Paris 2011
p. 8: © Vik Muniz / ADAGP, Paris 2011
p. 8: © Dominique Derive
p. 8: © Robert Falk
p. 9: © Marc Quinn
p. 10: © Pierre Dmitrienko / ADAGP, Paris 2011
p. 14: © Luis Ferreira / ADAGP, Paris 2011
pp. 16, 17: © Jean-Claude Farhi / ADAGP, Paris 2011
pp. 18, 20: © Guy de Rougemont / ADAGP, Paris 2011
p. 19: © Nancy Graves Foundation / ADAGP, Paris 2011
p. 21: © Frans Krajcberg
p. 21: © Darbaud - info@darbaud.fr
p. 21: © 2011 Sam Francis Foundation, California / ADAGP, Paris
pp. 26, 27: © Calder Foundation New York / ADAGP, Paris 2011
p. 27: © Francesco Clemente
p. 27: © Fondation Pierre Bergé–Yves Saint Laurent
p. 34: *Dame en noir* © Alexandre Roubtzoff
p. 34: © Jean-Marie Fiori / ADAGP, Paris 2011
p. 38: © Marc Quinn
p. 38: © Claude Lalanne / ADAGP, Paris 2011
p. 40: © Nicholas Krushenick
p. 40: © Hubert Le Gall / ADAGP, Paris 2011
p. 41: © Alexandre Fassianos
p. 48: © Jacques-Emile Blanche / ADAGP, Paris 2011
p. 62: © The Andy Warhol Foundation for the Visual Arts, Inc. / ADAGP, Paris 2011
p. 64: © Aki Kuroda / ADAGP, Paris 2011
p. 86: © Jean-Claude Farhi / ADAGP, Paris 2011
p. 88: © Dominique Derive
p. 94: © Succession Picasso 2011
p. 94: © Dominique Derive
pp. 106, 108, 135: © Luis Ferreira / ADAGP, Paris 2011
p. 140: © A. Stickvey
p. 157: © Calder Foundation New York / ADAGP, Paris 2011
p. 157: © Calder Foundation New York / ADAGP, Paris 2011
p. 157: © Calder Foundation New York / ADAGP, Paris 2011
p. 160: © Dominique Derive
p. 160: *Spiegel* © Anne Neukamp
p. 161: *Napule* © Anne Neukamp
p. 161: © Aki Kuroda / ADAGP, Paris 2011
p. 161: © Aki Kuroda / ADAGP, Paris 2011
p. 161: © Dominique Derive
p. 164: *Foule* © Machat
p. 164: © Dominique Mercy / ADAGP, Paris 2011
p. 165: *Foule* © Machat
p. 166: © Successió Miró/ ADAGP, Paris 2011
p. 166: © Marco del Re
p. 166: © Successió Miró/ ADAGP, Paris 2011
p. 166: © Aki Kuroda / ADAGP, Paris 2011
p. 166: © Sergio Giral Jr., visual artist and photographer
p. 166: © Sergio Giral Jr., visual artist and photographer
p. 167: © Marco del Re
p. 167: © Aki Kuroda / ADAGP, Paris 2011
p. 167: © Kasimir Malevitch
p. 169: © Aki Kuroda / ADAGP, Paris 2011
p. 169: © Aki Kuroda / ADAGP, Paris 2011
p. 170: © Takis / ADAGP, Paris 2011
p. 170: © Calder Foundation New York / ADAGP, Paris 2011
p. 171: © Georges Braque / ADAGP, Paris 2011
p. 172: *Mr O* (5 ft. 3 in. x 2 ft. 7 ½ inches [160 x 80 cm]) © Christophe Raynal - www.christoperaynal.com
p. 172: © Aki Kuroda / ADAGP, Paris 2011
pp. 176, 178: © Marco del Re
pp. 176, 178: © Estate of Roy Lichtenstein New York / ADAGP, Paris 2011
p. 178: © Jean-Claude Farhi / ADAGP, Paris 2011
p. 180: © Estate of Roy Lichtenstein New York / ADAGP, Paris 2011
p. 180: © Estate of Roy Lichtenstein New York / ADAGP, Paris 2011
pp. 182, 183, 184, 185: Series *La Faune marine* © Vincent Leray
p. 191: *Looking Out to Sea, Tangiers* © Emile Wauters
p. 194: *Le reclute*, 1882 © Alberto Pasini
p. 199: *Serviteur en tenue de fête*, 1876 © George Willoughby Maynard
pp. 213, 215: *The Qur'am Lesson* © Johann Victor Kramer
p. 230: © Vik Muniz / ADAGP, Paris 2011
p. 232: © Christian Maas
p. 234: © Arman / ADAGP, Paris 2011
p. 242: © Sophia Vari
p. 243: © Sophia Vari
pp. 244-245: © Sophia Vari
pp. 246, 247: *Gouache tantrique* © Roger Van Rogger
p. 247: *Gouaches* © Roger Van Rogger
p. 248: © Lenka Beillevert
p. 248: © Ludovic Alussi
p. 249: © Ludovic Alussi
p. 254: © Calder Foundation New York / ADAGP, Paris 2011